Blogging

*The Best Darn Little Guide To Starting A
Profitable Blog*

Isaac Kronenberg

Table of Contents

A Free Bonus For You

As a thank you for purchasing this book, I have decided to throw in a free bonus for you. This bonus, an amazing little WordPress plugin, has the capability to help you take things up a notch with your blog.

You can find information on where to download this plugin in Chapter 17, and an explanation of how I recommend you use the plugin in Chapter 18.

While this plugin is not essential, I have found it to be very effective at what it does, and I think you'll find it to come in quite handy as another tool in your monetization arsenal. I hope you like it. Enjoy!

Introduction

Just who am I and why should you learn about blogging from me?

I'm a 40 year old entrepreneur from New York who used to work at a well-known Fortune 50 tech company, and decided to drop out of the corporate grind to work on my blog full-time.

Previously, I had been working on my blog for years for the pure enjoyment of it, and had amassed quite a large following, and when I decided to drop out of the workforce I had only just then figured out that I could monetize my blog, and did so as quickly as possible.

Upon making the shift to monetize my blog, I immediately started earning an income so large that it allowed me the freedom to quit my job and work on blogging full-time.

Blogging now pays me much more than my full-time salary ever did, and I now own not just one blog, but numerous blogs, which are all profitable I might add.

Since monetizing my blogging and seeing vast improvements in my lifestyle as a result, I've had many ask me to help them out with their blogs to get them to the same level as me, and so I started a blog consultation service to help others with their blogs.

I've helped all kinds of people with their blogs, from college students who just wanted to start a blog for the first time and obtain a part-time income, to executives in Fortune 500 companies. Most of the executives I helped already had blogs, but wanted to overhaul their clunky-looking out-of-date blogs into something more sleek and well-polished that truly represented their high level of expertise and experience, as well as figure out how to monetize things.

Case in point, I'd inadvertently become that go-to guy in the blogging world who knows how to take a small so-so little blog and get it up to the point where it's a highly profitable money making machine.

What separates this book from other blogging books?
Well, I've read all the other blogging books, and they all teach you how to blog, and teach you strategies for earning a profit, which is all fine and dandy. I'm not disacknowledging the other blogging books, as they all do teach something of value (well, maybe not all). However, I believe what separates this blogging book from the rest is that I've taken all of the most effective blogging monetization strategies gathered over my years of blogging and consulting others on their blogs, and have put it all into one great book. This book!

The book that you hold in your hands is the culmination of my many years of blood, sweat, and tears blogging, where I reveal to you all of the down and dirty secrets, all of the knowledge that I had obtained in this area, that if implemented correctly will take your blog from a hobby to a fully monetized beast! Or if you've never started a blog before, then this book will provide you with everything you need to know to help you get started on the right foot, and monetize your efforts right from the start!

Sure, I know you've heard it all before, just pick the right niche, write good articles, sprinkle affiliate links everywhere, and you are sure to make a profit.

Well, have I got news for you! That's NOT what the big money bloggers are doing! Though that's not to say there isn't some truth in the fact that putting affiliate links in your blog is part of the equation, but just sprinkling them around and hoping someone clicks on them is the wrong strategy entirely.

Thus, this book aims to reveal to you exactly what the big money bloggers really do (which is exactly what I do). Make no mistake about it, most who get into blogging are totally clueless in the area of monetization, and fail to make their blogs profitable, and since that is the reality of things, your competition is very low if you do things the right way, the way I illustrate in this book.

I would therefore like to reiterate that this book is not a book that will merely teach you how to simply get a blog up, though that part is covered as well. What this book truly is, is a book that will teach you how to obtain an income from your blog! So if making an income from your blog is what you are after, then you're definitely in the right place.

First of all, I'd like to state that in order to make real money blogging, there are 2 critical factors that matter above all else:
1. You are motivated to make money in the arena of blogging.
2. You implement the right strategies.

I'm sorry to say that this book is not the book to help you with your motivation, as you can find some other motivation guru for that, there are plenty of them out there. That being said, I do motivate the students which I mentor (because my reputation hangs on their success), and if you were interested in my mentorship program, I have information about that in Chapter 19 of this book. Though you don't really need my mentorship program if you simply follow the method explained in this book.

One point though, do not deviate from the method, as it's been proven and tested, and simply works. Occasionally, I have a student who has claimed that they followed my method and their blog was not making money, and after analyzing their blog I found out they they had left out a critical component, and when I asked why they had left out that component, they'd come back saying that they wanted to try this other thing. Well, that's why it didn't work, you didn't follow the method and want to try some other thing. I'm all for experimentation and all, but I strongly insist that you do follow the method and do not deviate from it until you are indeed making money from your blog!

Once your eyes are open to the reality what it takes to monetize a blog, then there is little to stop you from executing on that at much higher level and earning a full-time income off this, but you do have have to execute!

Perhaps you've been trying to monetize your blog and have picked up other blogging books, and all of those other blogging books failed you, and that's why you're here reading this book! Or maybe this is the first blogging book you've ever picked up, because you heard that what's taught in this book actually works. Or perhaps you're new to the whole blogging scene and something compelled you to want to start a blog, and so you picked up this book to learn about it. Or perhaps you're already an advanced blogger, and earning a full-time income off of what you do, and looking for some updated information to help you take your blog to the next level. Well, no matter where you are on the blogging totem pole or how you got here, I can assure you that this book will set you straight, putting you on the right track to crafting a blog that earns a rock solid income.

In fact, you'll never need to pick up another blogging book again after this book is through with you, because you'll know exactly what you have to do to monetize your blog. Trust me on this, this book will be the best blogging book you will have ever read on blogging, and it will show you a very true, very straight forward map to ensure that you get paid from your blog. The only way you can fail is by not implementing the method that I teach, so be sure to not just read this book passively and actually implement the method that I'm teaching you, as I'm absolutely certain that it works.

So sit back, relax, and put your reading glasses on if you've got them, because we're about to dive into the deep end of this whole making money with blogging thing full swing!

Chapter 1: A Word About Niche

When you create a blog, you need a niche, and if you don't already have one, then now is the time to start thinking about one.

There are entire books written about choosing a good niche, and while there is a certain science to finding a profitable niche, I strongly tend to disagree with the notion that earning money with a blog is all about finding a profitable niche. Anyone who is telling you this is filling your head with utter nonsense. As you'll soon learn, the niche you choose is largely irrelevant.

What I teach is that you write your own blog, and you write it from your heart. You should be open, honest, as transparent as possible, and you provide your audience with a highly sincere level of value that they can't get anywhere else. This is the true key to maintaining a following and to earning a profit with your blog.

The reality is that the best niche for you to write about will always be the niche that you are most passionate about, something you love. If you truly love what you are writing about, then there is a very high chance that a bunch of other people out there will love it too!

Frankly speaking, you have a higher chance of being successful blogging about some niche that never seemed like it could be profitable if you are passionate about that niche, than if you try to pick some niche just based on the fact that you are targeting profitable keywords. The big money bloggers only blog about what they are highly passionate about, and so this is what I highly recommend that you do as well.

Look at it this way, if your true passion happens to be little yellow pebbles, then blog about little yellow pebbles. The more unique your niche is, the less competition you'll have, and if you're the only one with a solid blog on the topic, then you'll have no competition at all. Though that doesn't mean that you should avoid blogging in niches that may seem oversaturated, as the reason that many niches seem to be oversaturated is because there is a very large audience in those niches who can't get enough of the information they crave, so there is plenty of room for many more bloggers to jump in and capitalize on that traffic. Though, the reality is that only the bloggers who are the most passionate about what they are blogging about will be able to acquire a long-term dedicated following, which is the goal that you should be striving for with your blog.

There are bloggers out there making a full-time salary writing in the most insane niches that you may have never even realized a profit could be earned from, so if you're truly passionate about little yellow pebbles and really want to write about them, then my answer to you would be: Well, you seem very passionate about it, so you definitely have a winning niche there!

Niche truly does fail to be an issue if you have something that you are totally, heads over heels, ultra-passionate about. And if you don't have that, then you need to think a lot harder in order to figure out exactly what you are really passionate about, because the reality of the situation is that if you don't have something that you're totally passionate about, then you don't really have a blog worth writing.

Any blog you create about something that you are not passionate about is not going to get you very far in the blogging world, and is doomed to fail, unless your only aim is targetting cheap traffic for short-term profit, but such a blog won't be sustainable in the long-term, so why waste your time with something unsustainable.

I mean, let's face the facts, if you create a blog, you're going to have to write blog posts regularly, and writing is already hard work as it is, and writing about something you just kind of feel so-so about is going to seem more like more of a chore compared something that you are totally excited to be writing about.

Thus, you really have to take a liking to what you are blogging about. Think about what a miserable existence you would have if you regularly blogged about a topic that you truly have no interest in whatsoever, would you enjoy that? How long could you do it for? Week? Months? Years? The chances are that such a pursuit would cause you to eventually quit blogging altogether, and never come back to it.

And so, I hope this chapter clarifies the whole question of niche, in that you need to blog in the area that you are the most passionate about. If you're not passionate about anything, then your job should be to put your blog on hold, put down this book, and find your passion first. Once you've found your passion, you're then ready to start your blog.

Because let's face it, you're going to be writing about your niche a lot, and so it must be something you actually like, and even better is if it is something that you truly love! No matter what any niche analysis expert tells you, this is the truth of the matter.

To drive this point home even further, let's take a look at the stock market, which is nothing more than a list of companies in different niches. Does anyone know which stocks will go up or down, or which company will be successful or fail? Despite all of the expert analysis and empirical data on the matter, not one of the experts can claim to really know.

Though no one can deny the fact that the companies that are most successful in the long-term are those companies where the people who run them are truly passionate about the product or service that their company provides, and blogging is no different, since the bottom line of blogging is that your blog is a company.

You heard me right the first time, your blog is a company! Don't make the mistake of thinking that it isn't! Even if it's not turning a profit yet, the moment you earn your first commission, you're suddenly a company. Even if you try to argue that you're not a company, if your blog is monetized and earning a profit, then I can guarantee that the tax authorities won't believe your "my blog is not a company" story.

And so, in the fashion of all great companies, you want to start off on the right foot by starting something great from the get-go with your blog, and this means that having passion for what you're going to be blogging about is the single most important defining element of success for you.

What is the reason most blogs fail? Because the people who started them were not passionate enough about their blogs, and decided to give up and do something else. Don't let that be you!

Let's not fool ourselves, passion is everything in this business! So no matter what your niche may be, it should be that thing that you feel most passionate about, and if it isn't then you're setting yourself up for failure, as well as a completely empty existence.

I could go on and on about why it's important that you blog about something that you are extremely passionate about, so rather than go on and on about it, I leave you with this final thought: If you read some random person's blog about a niche you happen to like, will you continue to read it if it was written with a ton of passion behind it (even if the writing itself is not so spectacular)? How about a similar blog in the same niche written by someone with an equal level of writing skill who just didn't seem so passionate about it at all? I think you know the answer, and based on that I rest my case.

Thus, I hope you are one of the lucky ones who knows what you are passionate about and doesn't have to put this book down to think about it. Because without having a passion, there really isn't any point

14

in moving forward. So if you don't have a passion, then please do us all a favor and put this book down and start thinking about it, and come back when you have one.

What should your niche be? It should most definitely be what you are most passionate about!

I hope this is clear!

Chapter 2: What Is An Affiliate Link?

If you think you know what an affiliate link is then I give you permission to skip this chapter and move on, although you might want to skim through it just a bit, because you might learn something.

However, if you don't know what an affiliate link is, then this chapter is for you.

An affiliate link in its purest sense is a link that a company provides you with which goes directly to a sales page of one of the company's products, and if that product is purchased, then the person who owns the affiliate link gets paid a percentage of that purchase by the company.

As a blogger, if someone finds an affiliate link on your blog and clicks it, it takes them to the sales page of the company. If they like what they see on the sales page and buy the product, then the company is informed through the magic of their affiliate link tracking system that the sale came from you, and as a result they'll pay you a percentage of the sale. This is a concept that's very important to wrap your head around, as affiliate links have risen to be the vehicle of choice by which most bloggers earn a profit.

Many companies have their own affiliate programs, and searching in any search engine for a keyword in almost any niche followed by the words "affiliate program" will most likely allow you to find an affiliate program in that niche, depending on the niche.

In addition to many companies having their own affiliate programs, there are several large companies called affiliate networks. These affiliate networks are in the business of managing affiliate programs for various kinds of businesses.

Any business can use an affiliate network to create their own affiliate program without needing their own affiliate link tracking system, and anyone can search an affiliate network to find an affiliate program they'd like to promote.

Thus, affiliate networks are very powerful platforms which allow bloggers and affiliate marketers to have a place where they can easily search for affiliate programs in whatever niche they desire and register for them without having to input their contact information or banking details again, all from the comfort of the affiliate network's website.

Affiliate networks have become so convenient, that many bloggers end up picking one of them, and never touching any affiliate program outside their affiliate network of choice. Thus, their paycheck every month comes from the affiliate network. I'm not the type of blogger who likes to put all of my eggs in one basket though, so I tend not to deal with just one.

Let's take a look at some of the affiliate networks out there. Though this is not an extensive list, some of the popular affiliate networks are:

CJ Affiliate by Conversant - Managing a large variety of affiliate programs, most of the affiliate programs here were created by larger companies and corporations. Therefore, the restrictions are very high for a business to get an affiliate program approved if you're not a large company.

Clickbank - Having a large variety of affiliate programs in a large variety of niches, most of the affiliate programs here are ones created by small businesses and sole proprietors. The restrictions here are fairly high to get an affiliate program approved.

JVzoo - This affiliate network focuses primarily only in the money making niche, but they take almost everyone. Their restrictions are low to get in, and basically nearly anyone can create an affiliate program with them.

Warrior Plus - Another affiliate network that focuses primarily on the money making niche, though not as large as JVzoo. While the restrictions are low to get an affiliate program approved, their approval process for products is a bit stricter than JVzoo, as they actually want to see your sales page to make sure it's not total junk.

Thus, when seeking to join an affiliate program, you have a choice of dealing with a company directly who has their own affiliate program managed by their own affiliate link tracking system, or dealing with one of the many affiliate networks out there. As for me, I deal with both.

And that's what an affiliate link is!

If it doesn't make complete sense yet, keep reading, because we're not done talking about affiliate links yet by a long-shot.

Chapter 3: Types of Blogs

Aside from writing a blog in a particular niche, there are a great myriad of types of blogs one can write. I have listed the categories below, but this list is not a limiting defining factor by any means, as there are many more types of blogs that I could list, and the possibilities of types of blogs that can be created are in reality endless.

Money blogs - Blogs focused on techniques for acquiring wealth, this could be a blog that tries to pick the stock market, or a blog that covers the various areas of running a particular type of business. The consistent theme here is that these blogs all focus on engaging in specified activities that will result in an increase in wealth. Most of the readers of these kinds of blogs have an interest in getting rich.
How does a money blog turn a profit?
A money blog will turn a profit by eventually selling products to the reader that correlate directly with the niche the blog focuses on (the sheer variety of money making niches is almost endless) and what the articles in the blog talk about. The products the blog tries to sell might be a video course or a book that the owner of the blog created explaining in detail a method for making making money, such as a how to make money in the stock market course, or it might be an affiliate product.

Tutorial blogs - These are blogs that show you how to do something, and are educational blogs. Though it may not all be only tutorials, a large percentage of the content that attracts readers to these kinds of blogs are indeed the tutorials. Readers continue to read these types of blogs to learn how to get better at something (the sheer variety of niches that tutorials for things could be written about is also nearly endless).
How does a tutorial blog turn a profit?
A tutorial blog will turn a profit by recommending products that will teach you how to do something in greater detail than the articles in the

21

blog. These product can be a video course or book made by the owner of the blog, or they could be affiliate products.

Travel blogs - These are blogs that focus on travel, where the blogger is a traveller and writes about his/her experiences and adventures in other lands. Travel blogs usually upload lots of photos. They might also write reviews of certain products related to travelling, such as certain pieces of travel gear that served them well.

How does a travel blog turn a profit?

The travel blog will usually make money off of some product the blog sells providing the reader with information that they could not get anywhere else (like a guidebook showing you where to buy the best best coconuts at the best price in Chiang Mai). The travel blog might also turn a profit by providing affiliate links for travel products that they review.

Lifestyle blogs - A lifestyle blog could indeed be a travel blog, or a money blog, or another kind of blog, and the line is gray as to what actually constitutes a lifestyle blog. However, a lifestyle blog generally is a blog that talks about and promotes living a particular type of lifestyle in which others are interested in (even if those who read the blog don't really live that kind of lifestyle themselves).

How does a lifestyle blog turn a profit?

As with the other types of blogs, a lifestyle blog turns a profit by trying to sell products related to a certain aspect of the lifestyle the blog is promoting. These products may be created by the owner of the blog, but are usually affiliate products.

Review blogs - A review blog is a blog that reviews products within a particular niche. For example a review blog might review notebook computers, and cover all the various kinds of notebook computers and have its own rating system for reviewing notebook computers. Each blog post will likely be a review of a new notebook computer that just came out.

How does a review blog turn a profit?

A review blog mostly makes money from the affiliate links provided on each product it reviews. A review blog might also come out with its own product related to the niche in which it reviews products in, but most of the money with a review blog tends to be earned from its affiliate links in its reviews.

There are many other types of blogs, and I'm not going to get into them all, but as we can see from this list, the way most blogs make money is by either selling their own products or promoting affiliate products, which means you need to get good at either one or the other, or both. I tend to engage in both!

Chapter 4: To Put Your Face On A Blog or Not

When you're just starting your blog, you have the option to put your face on it, or not put your face on it. What I mean when I say put your face on it doesn't necessarily mean putting a picture of you on your blog, but it means revealing your identity.

If you have a very reputable job, and if your passion is something that could detract from that reputable image, then putting your face on a blog is something that you might not want to do.

Thus, the choice to put your face on a blog or not is entirely personal.

Though I would say that if you can put your face on your blog and get away with it, it's much better. Since when someone puts their face on a blog, readers can feel that they are reading the blog posts of a real person, and thus trust can be built a lot faster. That said, this doesn't mean that you can't earn a profit with a blog that doesn't have your face on it, because you definitely can. Most of my blogs, for example, don't have my face on them, because I don't want others to know that I write them.

So as a rule of thumb, if your niche is something that you don't want other people knowing you're into, but you're passionate about it, then by all means blog anonymously under some pen name. Though if you can put your face on a blog and would feel no shame whatsoever about it, then by all means do so.

It's truly a personal choice if you want to put your face on your blog or not, and you should also consider the fact that if your blog's traffic were to suddenly skyrocket, do you really want everyone knowing who you are wherever you go?

Many bloggers with their face on their blog get recognized when they go out in public, and sometimes that can be a good thing if people like you, but sometimes it could cause problems if there are a lot of people out there who despise what you stand for.

The reality is that every blog has its share of those who hate everything the blogger stands for, so don't expect everyone to like you. As hard as it is to believe, even I have my fair share of haters, which is exactly why most of my blogs don't have my face on them.

Therefore, please use your best judgement when deciding whether you want people to know who you are or not. And if you do decide to put your face on your blog, then please do not tell people where you live, and if you must provide an address for something, be sure to get a PO Box or some similar-type mailbox that doesn't reveal where you actually reside.

Chapter 5: The Difference Between Bloggers And Affiliate Marketers

While bloggers might not consider themselves affiliate marketers, the reality is that bloggers are definitely affiliate marketers, but just one particular type of affiliate marketer, being the type who writes a blog.

There are many other types of affiliate marketers from Youtubers, to Webmasters, to anyone who posts affiliate links on various non-blog websites. And since this is not an affiliate marketing book, but a book on blogging, I'm not going to get into all the various ways affiliate marketing can be done (it's quite a bit), but instead we'll only focus on how bloggers should be doing affiliate marketing.

I would say though, that the moment you post your first affiliate link on a your blog, you suddenly become an affiliate marketer. However, you are still a blogger!

Don't change your label and call yourself an affiliate marketer, you should continue to proudly refer to yourself as a blogger!

Just because you engage in affiliate marketing doesn't mean you have to call yourself an affiliate marketer, even though the moment you put up that first affiliate link you actually are one.

As the art of pure affiliate marketing is not at all about blogging, and someone who blogs while engaging in affiliate marketing is not in the purest sense an affiliate marketer.

I mean if you think about it, to be a blogger you have to wear many types of hats (writer, web designer, reporter, business owner, etc.). So does it really mean that since you engage in all of those tasks that you suddenly have to accept all of those labels? Well, you do to some

27

extent, but if it's all in the name of blogging, then you're actually a blogger, and all the other hats you wear just kind of go with the territory of blogging.

The lines might blur as to what you really are at times, and it may sometimes seem like you're having an identity crises, but the good news is that as long as you believe in your heart that you are a blogger, then you will be a blogger! So keep believing! You are a blogger!

Chapter 6: Energy

Everything in the universe is energy, and as a human you are a happy little bundle of energy.

When you do anything such as blog, jog, talk, commute to work, take out the trash, etc., you are expending energy.

Without getting all spiritual on you, I want you to recognize the fact that you are actually a vessel of energy, and the world as we know it functions entirely on energy.

And as a blogger, you'll soon start to realize just how important energy becomes to you, as the energy you put into your blog will in many ways affect the success of your blog.

When I am working on my blog, I actually feel the energy drain out of me as I do everything that needs to be done on my blog, and during the act of blogging it becomes very apparent that there is actually an energy exchange going on here.

If you focus deeply and put all of your energy into your blog, the result will be that your blog will shine! However, if you create your blog half-heatedly, write your posts half-heartedly, and expect a high level of success, then you will be greatly disappointed.

Your blog is a creature needs your undivided attention and focus when you work on it. Think of your blog as your little virtual command center that you bond with and beam out large discharges of energy into on a regular basis.

If you start thinking of it in terms of discharges of energy from you to your blog, you'll survive a lot longer and be better in tune with what you need to do to get your blog working for you rather than you working for your blog.

You can't simply dish out energy into your blog non-stop. You have to sometimes take time away from your blog in order to recharge. Develop this habit and you'll be a happy, healthy blogger.

Though, the more energy you give your blog, the faster you'll see results, so be sure to give lots of energy to your blog on a regular basis, keep it nourished, and you will in the end be victorious. Just be sure to recharge yourself, otherwise you'll burn out big time.

Perhaps you've heard this all before, but be sure to eat right, and get out and walk around or jog a lot, putting some focus on your health as well. Too much blog and no sunshine can really be damaging to the body.

I only tell you all of this, because I have seen bloggers become so infatuated with their blog that they burn out and quit, or develop health problem as a result of being so utterly focused on their blog non-stop. Don't let this be you!

You need to take a break and recharge sometimes, do it for the long-term symbiotic relationship of you and your blog. Keep this in mind, because writing a blog is like getting married in many ways, and if you develop an unhealthy relationship with your blog, the end result of that won't be very pretty.

Chapter 7: Getting Started

So if everything I've said so far hasn't scared you away yet, and you're ready to continue, then it's definitely time to get started! Hooray!

For those new to blogging, you'll find everything you need to get started right in this chapter. For those not so new to blogging, maybe you want to skip this chapter.

There are certain technical tidbits you have to figure out when starting a blog, and those are:

1. Get a Domain Name from a Registrar
2. Get Hosting
3. Install WordPress
4. Learn WordPress

If you haven't delved into these areas or don't even know what WordPress is, then I'm going to try to make this as simple as possible for you so that we can get get the ball rolling on the important stuff, which is blogging for profit.

Since the packages (features, pricing, etc.) for hosting and registrars is constantly changing, it seems easiest to refer you to a page on my website which provides the most updated information of what I would recommend someone new to blogging get in order to get started with your blog as quickly as possible. And since this book is not a technical WordPress manual, on the same page on my website I also provide you with information on where and how to learn WordPress. Go here to check out this page:

BloggerBlogger.com/basics

Note: To view this page on my website, you'll have to put in your email which will add you to my list (which will provide you with the latest blogging industry news, the latest most updated blogging strategies, and the latest tools that big money bloggers use). You can read more about my list in Chapter 16. Though if you really don't want to be on my list you can at anytime unsubscribe, though I hope you you don't, so you have nothing to lose and everything to gain by joining.

Tasks to complete:
1. Sign up for hosting and get a domain name either from a domain registrar or as part of a package from the hosting company.
2. Figure out how to install WordPress, and install it.
3. Learn WordPress.

Chapter 8: Consistently Promote A Handful of Affiliate Links

I absolutely shudder every time I hear a blogging book mention that you just want to sprinkle affiliate links throughout your blog and that 's going to help you make money with your blog. No, no, no, no, no! It's just not done that way!

Sprinkling affiliate links everywhere won't hurt, especially if you're a lifestyle blogger, but if you want your blog to be truly profitable, then what you need to be doing is what the big money bloggers do!

So how do the big money bloggers profit from their blogs if they're not sprinkling affiliate links everywhere?

Big money bloggers are always continuously promoting somewhere from 3 to 5 affiliate links and nothing more, and if you analyze the blog of any big money blogger you'll see this. Sure, sometimes they throw some other odd affiliate links here and there (a little sprinkle here, a little sprinkle there), but this is not their main strategy. If you examine the blogs of most big money bloggers, you'll find that they are consistently promoting the same handful of products, and that these products are the most relevant to their readers.

If you're only going to promote a handful of products consistently, promoting only the most relevant products to your readers is absolutely critical to your success! Remember that always!

Are you saying that I don't have to go around joining a bunch of affiliate programs and that just 3 to 5 affiliate links will do?

Yes, that's exactly what I'm saying! You only need a 3 to 5 links and nothing more! However, they should be very good affiliate programs that you could continue to promote for years and years, which pay a very good percentage. Only you can be the judge of what a good percentage is, largely depending on what your niche is, the value of the product, and the conversion rate, but as a rule of thumb I would try to avoid any affiliate program that pays less than 30%.

That said, there are some big money bloggers who write review blogs, and review blogs are the only exception to this rule. If the purpose of your blog is to review products, then you want an affiliate link for every product you review. That said, you still want to have a few main products that you should be consistently be promoting, and you should not deviate from promoting that same handful of products. Even the big money review bloggers implement this strategy at some point, because it works. Though if your blog is a review blog, you could still earn a good sum of money without implementing this strategy, but implementing this strategy on a review blog would make it a truly well-monetized review blog!

Thus, the lesson here is that you want to makes sure that you have somewhere between 3 and 5 affiliate links that you always promote.

What you promote is highly relative to your niche, however make sure your main affiliate links that you consistently promote are something relevant that people will continue to need years down the road.

The logic of promoting the same products again and again is that people who keep reading your blog will eventually get used to seeing the same products that you are promoting over and over, and will at some point want to buy one of them, or all of them. It's an old psychological marketing trick, and it's highly effective. If you keep seeing a big name-brand of soda again and again, and have never tried it, at some point you're probably going to want to try it.

You want your 3 to 5 links to be not only links, but banners, if the affiliate program that you're signed with has banners (most affiliate programs do). Also, you want to put these banners on a part of your blog where they can be seen over and over, no matter which page of the blog someone goes to. I find the sidebar or footer area work best for this, or both!

But how do I even get affiliate links?

Method 1 - Search For Affiliate Programs In A Search Engine
Just search in any search engine for keywords in your niche followed by the keywords "affiliate program" and you're sure to find some affiliate programs.

Method 2 - Search For Affiliate Programs In Affiliate Networks
If method 1 doesn't work for you, then type the keywords "affiliate network" or type the names of one of the affiliate networks mentioned in Chapter 2 into a search engine, and then search that affiliate network's database for various keywords in your niche to see what they've got. Affiliate Networks usually rate affiliate programs in their database by conversion rate or by a ranking system called EPC (earnings per click), affiliate programs that rank high for one of these rating systems usually do better. Also, some affiliate networks will tell you the refund rate. As you can guess, you don't want to choose any affiliate programs with a high refund rate. One last number to pay attention to is the number of sales, if the affiliate program has an excellent conversion rate and EPC, and zero for a refund rate, but has only had one sale ever, then I probably wouldn't go with that program without more data behind it.

Ultimately though, the deciding factor for whether or not you should go with an affiliate program should be what you think of the sales page that the affiliate link goes to. If it's something you would buy based on the sales page, then I would say go with it. However, if the sales page makes you cringe, then definitely do not go with it.

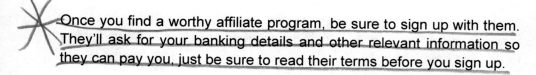

Once you find a worthy affiliate program, be sure to sign up with them. They'll ask for your banking details and other relevant information so they can pay you, just be sure to read their terms before you sign up.

If your niche is so obscure that you're still having trouble finding an affiliate program relative to your niche, then it's time to put on your creative thinking hat and think about what other things are indirectly related to your niche and search for those. Make a list of every affiliate program that you find that could be possible until you have a large list of affiliate programs, and choose the top ones out of those.

Lastly, be sure to get those banners on your blog somewhere where they can always be seen (such as your sidebar or footer). If that seems hard, consider all of those who gave up before you who couldn't figure that out. By figuring it out you've beat them! You savvy affiliate marketer you! I mean, you savvy blogger you!

Congratulations! You've just monetized your blog!

Hopefully, you took my advice and picked some really good affiliate marketing programs that will still be desirable years into the future. If you chose right you'll never have to go through that process ever again! Yippy!

One last word about affiliate links. Depending what country you're in, you want to check your country's laws regarding whether you need to disclose your affiliate links. The U.S. for example has very strict guidelines regarding the proper disclosure of affiliate links on any blog or website, and while I've never heard of any blogger getting caught for not disclosing affiliate links, the penalties for non-disclosure are quite hefty. If you're in the U.S., then I would like to urge you to check the Federal Trade Commission's guidelines on this at:

FTC.gov

If you're not in the U.S., then I urge you to check your own country's laws on this matter.

Super-Savvy Advanced Trick

Someone can just look at a banner of a product on your blog and open a new tab in their browser and buy it without ever clicking on your affiliate link, so one way to be sure people click on your link is to throw in a free bonus if someone buys the product through your link. You want to look at how other blogs implement this strategy to get ideas of how you could do it. That said, plenty of big money bloggers don't implement this trick at all and still make a killing, so it really depends on how super-savvy advanced you want to get with things!

Chapter 9: Get Your SEO Straight

Look, it's the year 2017, and SEO (Search Engine Optimization) now isn't what you thought it was. Though even as it continues to evolve, if you do what I lay out here, you should be totally fine no matter how the landscape changes.

The reality of SEO is that it's entirely controlled by Google these days, and they have gotten in a habit of penalizing any website that tries to game the system. How do they penalize you? With a lower search ranking of course!

Therefore, the old tricks of repeating keywords many times throughout your posts and putting a bunch a backlinks to your blog on spam sites doesn't work as well as it used to, especially if Google thinks for one moment that your are trying to game the system.

The best way to get ranked highly for your blog is to post often and post high quality original content. If your content is on-target with your niche, then the right keywords will naturally be in your content. So basically, the system that Google has devised for you to be able to rank your blog is a system where you shouldn't even be thinking about how to rank your blog, but rather you should be thinking about what great content you should be posting.

You don't need SEO! Trust me on this! You just need to be posting more, and posting high quality content that doesn't look like it's a page full of the same keyword. Forget even thinking about keywords entirely, and just focus on making your blog a good one!

There is no better strategy one could implement to get their SEO straight then to forget about SEO entirely. I mean let's face it, Google is a multibillion dollar company, not a caravan of fools. They know the tricks people have been doing to try to rank their blogs, and they're not going to have it anymore. Blogs are being penalized every day as we speak, for trying some sort of trickery to rank higher. It just doesn't work anymore! Google knows what you're doing!

Do you really think a multi-billion dollar company who wants blogs ranked based on post frequency, high quality content, and traffic is going to allow anyone to game to the system? Not anymore, and if some loophole in the system is found, you can be sure that it won't be long until Google kills that loophole and penalizes anyone who took advantage of it.

How often should I post?
Well, if you want to rank really well, then as often as you possibly can, but a few times a week should do! Or once a week at a minimum! The reality is that posting good content as much as you possibly can simply gives your blog more to rank for.

What Google really wants to see is original content (and they do actually check your content to make sure it's original) that is up-to-date and being posted as frequently as possible. Nothing is better in Google's eyes than a highly active blogger who keep on posting like a madman. If you really want to rank, that madman should be you! Post your heart out and don't stop posting for anything!

When you think about how to improve your SEO, just post another piece of content. It's really just that simple. You don't need to do much more than that to have your blog ranking highly. Keep doing it, and as the months go by, you'll see your blog start to rank.

Are you really telling me that all there is to ranking my blog is posting as much as possible, and that there are really no tricks to it?
Well, it wouldn't be completely honest of me if I told you that's all there was, but that is indeed most of it!

Though there are actually a few more things you need to do if you really want to rank well with Google. Remember when I said you didn't

40

need SEO. Well, you don't really need it, but there are still some things you should do, and here they are:

1. Register your website with Google Webmasters. You can find them at: Google.com/webmasters. Google Webmasters changes a lot, so check it often. Consider Google Webmasters to be the most important website that is going to help you with your rank. Most important is the Search Conole there. You want to add your website to it by clicking on "Add A Property." Then you want to verify your website with Google in at least one way, but it's much better for your ranking is to verify your website in all the ways that are possible, or in as many of them as you can. Google has tutorials on this stuff and much, much more. You want to click one by one on everything in the Search Console, and you want to get to know the Search Console very well, so be sure to bookmark it, and make sure your site's information is input into every single section of the Search Console that you are able to input something into. You don't have to be perfect, but try to understand as much as you possibly can about the Search Console and try to give Google as much information as they need to rank your website. Lastly, you want to try to ensure that you understand everything that Google wants you to do, so make sure you search in Google's search engine for "Google Webmaster Academy," and click the first link that pops up, and take those tutorials learning whatever new information Google wants you to know. Google is always changing things with Google Webmasters, so what I tell you here today could be outdated tomorrow, so it's good to keep checking Google Webmasters to see what's new!

2. Start a Youtube channel and under every video put a link to your blog. You should also put a link from your blog to your Youtube channel. If you've never heard of Youtube, you can find it at: Youtube.com. And guess what, you don't have to put your face on your Youtube videos, you can make a slideshow

41

presentation in Powepoint (or similar slideshow making software), export it as a video, and upload it to Youtube. Or you can just talk with your camera pointed at something interesting, and not show your face, and upload Youtube videos that way. The point is to put a link to your blog under every video. Youtube has its own tutorials and ranking on Youtube is another beast entirely, but well worth learning if your want your blog to seriously rank, so I recommend you get into it.

3. Set up a Google Plus profile and link that to your blog. Likewise, you should also be linking your blog to your Google Plus profile. Basically, you want to link everything to everything. You can find Google Plus at:
Plus.google.com

4. Make a Google Maps profile of your location, and link that to everything and link everything to that too. However, don't blame me if some crazy person finds you. If you're really worried about it, then you can leave this one out, or use a PO Box as your location. You can find Google Maps at:
Maps.google.com

You don't have to take all of these steps, but the first one is definitely essential. What you're basically doing with the other steps is creating properties on Google where everything is linked to everything, and thereby creating a Web of your content online between Google properties.

Google owns Youtube, and Google's other properties such as Google Plus and Google Maps are of course owned by Google, and they really want you to know about these properties and connect them to other properties, and they'll reward you with a higher search ranking if you do it. If you know of any other Google properties that I didn't mention or if any new ones come out (they keep coming out with more), then you want to register with those as well, and link them to your blog and to everything else too.

I hope having to learn about Google isn't making you rethink whether you even made the right choice in starting a profitable blog in the first place. Look, you have to do as much of this SEO stuff as you can, and keep working at it until you completely understand all about Google and all of their properties. It's exactly why they have tons of tutorials for you, because they want you to understand them!

Think of it this way, this is the barrier of entry that most blogs don't pass. If you do this stuff, I guarantee you're going to start ranking well! It seems harder than it is at first, but please do make sure to make a consistent effort to understand Google! It will be well worth your time, and your blog will greatly benefit from your effort!

Sure, you could also go ahead and link your Facebook and Twitter to your blog (and it will also help, so you definitely should do that too), but it won't have as much of an impact as linking Google owned properties, unless Google were to buy Facebook or Twitter sometime in the future.

Basically though, linking Google's other properties to your blog together with all of your other Google properties will blast your SEO to the moon. All this, and posting blog posts frequently. And if possible posting Youtube videos frequently too. And while you're at it, it wouldn't hurt to post on Twitter and Facebook frequently. You could actually make something called a Facebook Page, and post on that frequently and link that to your blog too, and link your blog to your Facebook Page!

One point about Youtube, the same way that I'm telling you to post frequently, because having an updated blog is important, well if you get into the habit of making Youtube videos, having an updated Youtube channel is equally as important. So make sure you put out at

43

least one Youtube video a week, and also make sure that one video is just over 10 minutes long (don't ask me why, but 10 minutes has become the sweet spot for ranking Youtube videos).

If all of this seems hard at first, it's because it is hard, but it's highly effective. Trust me, you need to do all of this! Or at least as much as you can!

I know this can all seem overwhelming, but it's one very important aspect of things. As mentioned, you don't have to do all of this, but the more you do the better off you are. At the very least, you need to do step 1! And then work on the the others.

Just make a little extra time each time you work on your blog to do something towards better SEO for at least 10 minutes or more, but keep posting as your main priority!

It might take some time, but once you get all of this stuff under your belt, you'll suddenly realize that SEO is the least of your concerns, and with your blog monetized to the teeth with affiliate banners, getting your SEO straight is going to definitely, 100%, without a doubt, put money in your pocket.

If you do all this, there is little more you have to do, because you're going to start to see an income from it!

Before you start freaking out at the sheer size of the mountain you've got to climb, just realize that no one ever fully conquers SEO, because the Internet keeps changing. What's important here is making an effort to consistently work at your SEO a little bit each time you post to your blog, for at least 10 minutes at a time!

And just try to relax, everyone freaks out when they realize how overwhelming all this SEO stuff is, which is why I didn't want to completely overwhelm you and get into the fact that you should also be linking your blog with Instagram, Pinterest, LinkedIn, and Reddit, amongst other things. Yes you want to link your blog to these too!

The reality is that the work involved in SEO is a job within itself, and many who do figure it all out sometimes fall in love with it and start their own SEO business where they just do SEO for other businesses all day, and charge them thousands of dollars a month for it, but that's completely the topic of another book, an SEO book.

Anyway, just 10 minutes after each post, do something to boost your SEO! You can do it!

And that's all we're going to cover on SEO!

But wait, there is actually more we have to do that's not SEO, so see you in the next chapter!

Chapter 10: Make Constant Improvements

Okay, so now that we've got your affiliate link money generating machine in place, and we've got you posting regularly with your little web of Google properties all connected, your next goal is to always be looking at how you should be making improvements to your blog.

Basically, once a week, or once a month at a minimum, you should be analyzing your blog and deciding on what could be improved, and then quickly implementing the improvement. It could be moving something to a different place in your sidebar, or changing a graphic, or whatever. The point is to be making an active effort over time to improve the look, feel, and overall usability of your blog.

If you have a new blog, it won't start out looking perfect at all, but keep posting and keep making constant improvements, and you'll soon find yourself with one super-cool, totally amazing blog that others often commend you on.

All the big money bloggers didn't get their blogs looking so fine overnight, it was a constant struggle of little improvements over time, a graphic change here, a color change there, a little tweak to this, a little splotch added to that; I think you get the idea.

Though make sure you take a very active approach to getting your blog to look and function as wonderfully as it possibly can. And if for any reason you start running out of ways that your blog can be improved, because it just looks so spectacular, well that's a problem we'd all like to have.

Chapter 11: Have A Sense of Purpose

Guess what? Blogging is a job! You're not just going to get there sitting on your behind waiting for something to happen, you're going to have to take massive action!

The fact is, that if you're not motivated to make something happen, and if you're not blogging with the belief that whatever you're blogging about is the greatest thing to happen to the the human race since the invention of fire, then you've got a sense of purpose problem.

You have basically got to believe with a sense of purpose, 100%, that what you're blogging about is absolutely critical. And you have to believe it deeply, with every single fiber of your being at the most extreme level, because if you don't buy the load of crud that you're peddling, then no one else will either.

Therefore, if your blog isn't absolutely spectacular by your own standards, then you'd better either make it spectacular, or tear the whole thing down and build a better beast.

The bottom line is that you've got to believe and utterly love your blog, as if it were the most sacred thing in the universe! If you're just not seeing your blog that way, then you have to make tweaks, either to your blog, or to how you view of your blog, until you are seeing things that way.

The big money bloggers all have a sense of purpose, and completely love their blogs! Therefore, so should you!

Chapter 12: Write To One Person

When you're writing your blog posts, you want to envision your ideal reader in your mind as being one person.

Let's say for example that I write a tennis blog about tennis balls. I want to imagine my ideal reader as a girl named Samantha with black hair about 5 foot, 7 inches tall, who is a little overweight, and has taken up tennis to get into shape. And I want to write to her.

Every blog post I write should be written with Samantha in mind. I'm trying to appeal to her and not anyone else. The effect that will be achieved by doing this is that I'm going to attract readers who are like the ideal person I'm trying to appeal to, and maybe a few other types of readers along the way. However, I'm targetting an ideal audience, and they'll love reading my blog, because no one else is writing to them except me.

Well, how do you choose an ideal person to write to?
You really have to sit down and think about who the ideal person is who reads your blog, and perhaps even make a profile of who they are, what they look like, what kind of job they might have, what their hobbies are, and why they like reading your blog. Once you have an image of your ideal reader clearly in your mind, you have someone to write too.

This really does make a difference, and all of the best bloggers implement this strategy. They write as if they're writing to one person, a close friend that they know, and this is what you need to be doing.

Sure, you don't have to do what I say, you can write your blog anyway you want. However, if you are serious about writing a blog that will actually pay you a full-time salary, you have to be able to captivate an audience of a particular niche and this is exactly how it is done. If you want to go your own way on this, then fine, but it's deviating from this method and not what the big money bloggers are doing.

Write to one person!

Chapter 13: List Building

Okay, if you're not a total newbie to this blogging thing, then you may have heard that the money is in the list. However, just because you have a list or have figured out how to build one doesn't mean that you're suddenly going to be rolling in the dough.

There is a bit of technique required to profit from your list, but first I'm going to give you a little background about autoresponders.

When I say the word autoresponder I'm talking about a service that manages a list of your subscribers and the emails that you send them.

Now, if you've never dealt with an actual autoresponder, then let me first of all put it in your head that some regular email service like Hotmail, Yahoo, or Gmail just won't do. You need something that can email mass amounts of people and have your email reach their inbox, and the reason is that you need the ability to write an email and with one click be able to send it to thousands of your subscribers without any problems.

Thus, you need an autoresponder. Now there is no best autoresponder, and they all have different price plans, advantages, and disadvantages, though some of the more popular ones are MailChimp, Aweber, and GetResponse. Though there are hundreds out there. The one I use you can find in the sidebar of my website at:

BloggerBlogger.com

If you're new to this building a list thing, then you're going to want to go with something like MailChimp, because MailChimp is free (be sure to read MailChimp's terms of agreement though, because they don't allow certain niches). However, as you start to build a list that goes over 50 subscribers, you might want to shop around.

How do I build a list?

That's a great question, and I'm glad you asked. Well, it could be as simple as just putting a form on your blog that says "join my list, enter your name and email here to subscribe!" However, that's a very basic way of doing things, and your list won't grow very fast that way.

The way the big money bloggers do it is that they offer something of value that they know their readers want, which they give to their readers in exchange for their email. This is usually a PDF document that has some vital piece of information that their readers want to know, but it could be anything that would have value to your readers. Back to the tennis example, you could offer your readers a report that lists the top 10 best tennis rackets, or something to that extent, something they'd be willing to give you their email for.

Whichever autoresponder service you go with, will have some code you can paste in your blog which will display a form that your readers can enter their email address into and click and submit button, and when your readers do this they'll get an automated email shot instantly to them from your autoresponder with a link to the report that you promised them. And from then on, they're on your list, although they could always unsubscribe if they don't like the emails you're sending them.

Once you get that right, you should have no problem at all getting some subscribers and growing your list. However, if you find that your blog is getting a lot of traffic, but not so much of that traffic is joining your list, then you perhaps need to rethink what you're offering them for their email, and offer them something better.

Once you start getting daily joins to your list, you're in good shape. However, that leaves you with a new problem, which is what to do with all of these people on your list?

What do I do with my list?

Another fabulous question! Well, you need to start emailing them. I recommend you email them 2 or 3 times a week. Basically, you want to notify them every-time you post a new blog post, and give them a little sales pitch as to why they should go to your blog and check it out. However, every now and then you want to email them some really valuable piece of information that only people on your list can get, because getting valuable information is the reason your readers will stay on your list and not unsubscribe, as you want to retain these people.

Also, every now and then you want to email your list an affiliate link to some product you really like (or really think they'd like), or some new feature or fact of one of those products you should be consistently promoting. This allows you to monetize your list!

Think of emailing your list as emailing that person who regards your blog as their most favorite blog whole wide world. You want to keep them happy as a subscriber on your list, and so you need to be hitting them with value consistently.

Now emailing a list is a bit of a different skill than writing a blog, but it's actually not that different, as it is writing. Though the goals of emailing your list should be:

1. To let your subscribers know when you post something new to your blog.
2. To give your subscribers key pieces of value that your blog readers who are not subscribed to your list won't get.
3. To promote your affiliate products to.

It takes some time to get things right, and the best way to learn is to find a bunch of top blogs and subscribe to the lists of those bloggers, and see how they do it. And what you'll find is that each of them has a different style, and does things a little differently, though they'll all adhere to the 3 goals I mentioned above.

You should learn as much as possible from how other bloggers email you when you're on their list, and from that you can see what you like and what you don't like about the way they email you. And with that knowledge, you want to start emailing your own list.

As I've said, it takes time to get it right, but keep at it, as emailing your list is one component of running a successful blog that you can't afford not to get good at.

I'd say after you write 200 or so emails to your list, you'll be a master of the list thing.

Note: Do not send your list so many emails to the point that your spamming them, or you're likely to get a lot of unsubscribes. You're trying to win the hearts of your subscribers, so you want to put yourself in their shoes. Just try to stick to twice a week, or perhaps 3 times a week, and you should be fine. Though every now and then someone will unsubscribe, but don't let it get to you, it's all a part of the game!

Chapter 14: The Roadmap To Success

Let's go over the roadmap to success:

Step 1. Set up your blog so it's looking nice, and so you can write posts..

Step 2. Find somewhere between 3 to 5 affiliate products that relate to your niche that you can consistently promote, and put their banners either on your sidebar or footer, or both.

Step 3. Post regularly, and work to improve your SEO consistently.

Step 4. Make little continuous improvements to your blog.

Step 5. Get an autoresponder, and give away something of value in exchange for emails, so you can build a list.

Step 6. Email your list consistently with as much value as possible.

That's pretty much the whole process in a nutshell. If you have that going, there is really not much else you can do.

Well, actually I'd be totally lying to you if I told you there is not much else you can do, as there is one more piece of the pie you should be looking at.

You basically need to accept the fact that everyone who writes a blog is doing all of these things (actually, most are not doing all of these things), so you need to have yourself some advanced strategies, and that's what the whole next section is about. The advanced strategies that will really take you to the top.

Chapter 15: Advanced Strategies

Congratulations on getting a working blog going and posting like a champ, keep at it and you're sure to have full-time income in no time. However, there is a bit more we can do if you want to really monetize this thing all the way!

Make Your Own Product
The reality of the situation is that you can just earn a full-time salary off affiliate links alone, however you'll notice that all of the big money bloggers in addition to putting affiliate links on their blog are also selling their own product. Now, if you haven't done everything else mentioned in this book, I would say that you are not ready to create your own product yet. However, if you have done everything that this book states to do so far, and the the growth of your blog is well under way, then it's high time you create your own product.

Your product can be a variety of things, depending on the niche that you're in, though what the big money bloggers generally sell are four types of things.
1. Software
2. Courses
3. Coaching/Consulting services
4. Physical Product

If your blog is about something technical and if there is a software that doesn't exist that can benefit your readers, then you should make it. Though you don't have to program it yourself. What you should do is go on a site like Freelancer.com or Upwork.com or any other website where you can hire a programmer, and hire one to build you a piece of custom software that you can sell for 100% profit.

If you can't think of any software that your audience would need, then there is sure to be something that you can teach your audience that you can make a course about and be able to charge for it. Your course can be in the form of a written PDF report, or it could be a video course, or even better would be a video course membership website (a site that people pay to join either for a one time fee or a monthly payment, which contains a video course that is regularly updated, where new videos are added monthly and possibly has a forum or Facebook group attached to it), but it should be something that your audience is willing to pay to learn about. If something like that exists in your niche, then you're golden.

The next product that you can sell is basically yourself. If you are so knowledgeable about your niche that you can offer some type of coaching or consulting service for the right price, then you want to list out what your service is and how much you charge for it, and you'll find yourself getting a few clients here and there, or being so overbooked with clients that you don't have time to work on your blog (problems we like to have).

Lastly, if your niche is the kind of niche where you could sell a physical product to them, then you'd better start thinking about how to manufacture and sell a physical product to them, or how to buy something at a wholesale price and set up an online store, or even better, how you could design a physical product and have it automatically drop-shipped to them.

While the big money bloggers can live just fine off of affiliate link money, they actually make a killing off selling their own products, and you want to capitalize on this too, even if it's as simple as creating a report.

Now, what's involved in making a product warrants a book of its own, so I'm not going to get into it here, as it is an advanced strategy which largely depends on what kind of product you intend to make and sell, though there is a plethora of free information on the Web about how to make a product. And an even more advanced strategy would be if you registered an affiliate program for your own product on a site like

JVzoo, and then got some affiliate marketers in your corner to market the product for you.

Though the reality is that posting to your blog consistently and promoting affiliate links is all you really need to do for a job replacing income. So if you're already doing that, then you don't have to do anything else. However, if you're already successful at that, and you are starting to think that it's time to do something more for bigger money, then you should definitely explore this side of things further, because it's the most profitable side of things actually, which is exactly why the big money bloggers are doing it.

WordPress Plugins
As a blogger who uses WordPress that is trying to make their blog profitable, there should be no surprise to you that there are actually a ton of plugins out there which can do certain things that can give one a major advantage over other bloggers.

While it hasn't been proven that you need plugins to run a successful blog, the big money bloggers all use them, and I happen to use them as well (I'm actually stacked to the teeth with all of the most advanced blog monetization plugins if you want to know the truth). And I've found that for myself, having an array of various plugins in my arsenal really does make a difference, so I'd highly recommend getting into plugins if you're not into them already!

I actually happen to be a regular connoisseur of WordPress plugins, and I'm especially into those plugins that can make blogs more profitable, so if you'd like to hear some more about what plugins I really like and why I like them, then I'd highly advise you to join my list, which brings us to our next chapter!

Chapter 16: Join My List

I'll tell you why you should join my list, it's because each of you who joins my list will get one million dollars just for joining! Just kidding!

What my list can realistically offer you is the latest blogging industry news, the latest most updated blogging strategies, and the latest tools (like plugins) that big money bloggers use. Thus, by joining my list you would be acquiring an edge over other bloggers by being tapped into the the heart of blogging know-how.

What better list to join when you're trying to get your blog to take off, than one written by the biggest blogging enthusiast (myself) on the face of the planet, whose only mission in life is to be a master of, and be on the up and up of single everything thing related to blogging. Trust me, it pays to have an utter blogging freak like myself on your side, so I look forward to having you onboard.

Don't worry though, I won't spam you, as I only email my list with high quality information related to blogging, so you should consider the act of joining my list as being an extension of this book, and part of the path to learning more advanced blogging strategies. Rest assured that all of your information will be kept confidential, and if you tire of my list you can always feel free to hit the unsubscribe button.

To join my list, all you need to do is get your free bonus mentioned in the next chapter. To the next chapter!

Chapter 17: Your Bonus

FREE PLUGIN

First of all, I'd like to give you your promised bonus, which can be found at:

BloggerBlogger.com/bonus

You'll need to enter in your email to unlock the page, which will give you access to your bonus, while at the same time adding you to my list.

What this bonus is, is a WordPress plugin that will help you to make money with your affiliate links, especially for products that you review or products that are your own. Instructions as to how to use this plugin can be found in the plugin itself by clicking the HELP button.

My only condition is that you may use this plugin to help you to make money with your blog, but you are not allowed to sell or giveaway the plugin.

The next chapter explains how to use the plugin.

Chapter 18: How To Use The Plugin

I'm assuming that you've installed and taken a look at the plugin, and watched the help video to understand how to use it.

It's pretty self explanatory how to use the plugin after watching that help video, but what should you really be doing with this plugin?

What I have found to be the most effective way to use this plugin is when I either release a new product or when I promote a new product that someone else has released.

Usually when I or one of my affiliates partners releases a new product, there is a launch phase where the product is heavily discounted, which is usually a day or a few days, so what I will do is make a page for that product on my website, explain about the product on that page, put the countdown timer on that page, and set the countdown timer to hit zero the moment the discount expires.

What this does is create a scarcity effect, where the person has to make a decision if they really want the product then and there, otherwise the price will go up, and I've ran split tests on this, and using that little countdown timer has lead to more conversions (more sales) for me than not using that countdown timer. So it really does work to increase conversions.

I've searched for other plugins that are better that do the same thing, but this is the best one I've found, and I absolutely love it!

I hope you see the value in it, and that you love this plugin as well. And now with some knowledge as to what to do with this plugin, you can can hopefully increase your conversions with it and make your money back on the money you've put down for this book!

If you have joined my list, then you're likely to see me use this strategy in certain situations when I announce the launch of a new product, so please do pay attention to what I'm doing when I do this!

Chapter 19: Beyond This Book

MENTORSHIP PROGRAM

For those interested in going well beyond the teachings of this book and really taking their blog to the next level, I do offer a private mentorship program where I analyze your blog and tell you exactly what you need to do to get it up to par, and push you to see that you do it.

Though please note that my mentorship program is limited to time-frames when I am taking new students.

To find out more about my mentorship program, and if I'm currently taking students, go to:

BloggerBlogger.com/mentorship

Note: My mentorship program is only for those utterly dedicated bloggers who truly want to take their blog to the next level, so if you feel that this is indeed you, then I look forward to mentoring you!